Made in the USA
Thornton, CO
12/11/23 09:40:35

3f0bec98-bb8f-4aee-8ecc-4ac01445ebcdR01